Poems from the Heart to the Soul

By Gia Schön

WTL INTERNATIONAL

Poems from the Heart to the Soul

Copyright © 2019 Gia Schön
Artwork by Gia Schön; author photo by Sabrina Savoy

All rights reserved. No part of this publication may be reproduced in any form or by any electronic or mechanical means including information storage and material systems, except in the case of brief quotations embodied in critical articles or reviews, without permission in writing from its publisher, WTL International.

Published by
WTL International
930 North Park Drive
P.O. Box 33049
Brampton, Ontario
L6S 6A7 Canada
www.wtlipublishing.com

978-1-927865-53-8

Printed in Canada and in the U.S.A.

Dedication

To my son Ben: you are the reason my heart keeps beating.

To Erminia, Melanie and Christina, my true soulmates: you were by my side in my darkest hours and stood by me as I found my way to the light. I am forever grateful!

To John and my mom Lucy:
thank you for your heartfelt love and support.

To Dr. Mungal and Mr. R. Roopa:
Thank you for helping me find me!

To all the souls who have suffered and felt alone at one time: these writings are for you to know you are not alone.

Those who may benefit most from this book:

- Anyone who has experienced a life trauma
- Anyone who lacks self-confidence
- Anyone who has experienced a broken heart
- Anyone who is in love
- Anyone who has lost a love
- Anyone who feels like no one understands

This is Me

Be true to you, and all will fall into place. This is me!

No filter is required—I am who I am. Some days are a struggle, some come easier than others.

I am not perfect—far from. The Lord knows I made many mistakes.

I am not the prettiest nor skinniest woman in the room, definitely not the smartest nor the most confident. Though extremely stubborn at times, make no mistake, I will jump hurdles for those I love. An introvert for the most part; I hide in corners at functions or keep myself distracted at times just to avoid interaction. Once you get to know me and I feel comfortable with you, you will wish I had remained the quiet girl in the corner, but I will always give you my heart.

I never confided in my family or friends of the doubts, the hurt, the feelings of loneliness, and the constant desire for isolation whirling in my mind. Thoughts of how I was ugly, fat, not good enough, how I did everything wrong, how no one liked me, wishing I could die are only a few of the many thoughts constantly overwhelming me. I would either stay quiet or put on a happy face and act like everything was okay. If I was out, I couldn't wait to go home and lock myself in my room to be alone and solitary.

Those closest to me knew something was wrong, but they couldn't figure out what the problem was. They asked me to seek a doctor's help, but I was afraid and would tell them to leave me alone, distance myself from them, or self-sabotage the relationship. *They just don't understand* or so I thought. Imagine my shock when I realized I was wrong…many of them did see the big picture, and the ones who truly mattered did understand.

Like many, I suffer from anxiety and depression. I suffered for many years behind closed doors till one day I finally broke. Unable to function, I found myself sobbing on the floor curled up in a fetal position. I knew I had no choice; it was time to get help. The time had come to ignore the stigmas and ignore what people would say; it was time to FIX ME.

After finding the right medication and many countless hours of therapy, which I still attend, I am a continued work in progress. Seeking help was inequitably the best decision I ever made.

Through therapy and self-reflection, I discovered much about me. Most importantly, I found out I am not the only one who suffers. "I am not the only one. Imagine that!" Others in the world suffer just like I do. What an eye opener to find out I wasn't alone! Others feel and understand what I am feeling.

I have an amazing family and friends who uphold me, yet I still feel alone most of the time. Then one day I wrote a poem and drew a picture to go with it. I was amazed when I was done—not because I liked what I wrote or drew but because of how it made me *feel!* I felt every kind of emotion, but the best one was the feeling of relief. So, I continued to write and draw…

And before I knew it, I was expressing myself through the poetry and art—talents I forgot I had. In elementary school, I remember writing poems and presenting them, and the "smart" kids would taunt me, saying, "No way you wrote that!" "You must have copied it from somewhere." "You are not smart enough to write something like that!" When I drew pictures in art class, the teachers made comments about how horrible my drawings were. That's all it took. I buried the art and poetry so deep I forgot all about them.

I am always trying to find and bring out the good in people along with myself. Far from perfect, many have I hurt, broke hearts, and had my own heart shattered. Not proud of many actions, but I have learned and continue to learn from my mistakes.

I started sharing my poetry on social media groups. Before I knew it, people from all walks of the earth began reaching out to me because they were able to relate to my words. My poetry resonated with them! As I listened to their stories, I would be so moved by their sharing that before I knew it, the words would just start flowing. Whether the story was about me or the person who had reached out, I simply wrote. I was able to capture in words what they were feeling deep down inside.

I realized it does not matter if the people with whom I was communicating were drug addicts, alcoholics, agoraphobes, or just everyday people who pretended everything was copacetic and chose to suffer quietly behind closed doors; we all suffered. Just like me, they felt alone.

We all might have chosen to handle our situations differently due to our unique circumstances or taken various avenues to find healing. In the end, it does not matter; we all suffered alike and would do anything to numb the pain. No human is the judge and jury alone; not a one of us is better than the other as we all have our inner demons to combat. Let's help one another defeat them and allow our inner angels to shine brightly!

I have learned and continue to learn to accept who I am!

Love and believe in yourself.

Gia Schön

Poems from my heart...

My Creed to Me

Every fall grounds me,
Every fall teaches me,
Every fall reveals my resilience,
If I make the mistake of falling flat on my face,
I will always get back up and rejoin the race.
I may struggle,
I may trip,
I may fall behind,
If needed, I will take a moment,
But make no mistake—
I will win the race
At my own pace!
I will embrace the faults,
I will embrace the thoughts,
I will embrace the silence,
I will always learn from the lesson:
I promise never to neglect—
Always reflect in honor
To run and win the next race.

 Somber Beauty

Watering one's soul—
Without the rain, there will be no flowers to bloom.
The tree leaves change along with the seasons;
They fall to allow the new.
Roots continue to grow stronger, yet the beauty of a tree's leaves will always return.
Water your soul; allow your soul to bloom;
Don't overlook your own inner beauty.

Have Faith; Release the Inner Spirit!

You hold the key—
Let it release the inner being we all see.
Allow yourself to release the pain;
Holding it truly has nothing to gain—
The body will set into depression.
Take from it the lesson;
It was a blessing, so stop guessing.
The aura surrounding you is starting to bloom,
So dig deep! Feel it in the womb—
The rebirth of a new you
On the rise—just release the ties!

Watching the Stars Sparkle So Bright

Words of wonder in my head...
Tears flow,
Smiles fade.
Every darkness brings a new beginning;
Beauty goes beyond one's dreams.
Pay attention as even on the darkest night
The stars sparkle bright,
And the sun will rise again.

Some Days You Just Want to Run Away

When you don't want to see,
Feel, or be a part of anything…
When all you want to do is hide
The person in the mirror…
You no longer recognize
Who's staring back…
Ignore what he or she has to say.
Soar the sky,
Use your wings,
Watch the tide,
And trust you will get on track.
Soon it will be nothing more than a flashback!
As hard as it is, start with a crawl
Till you are able to stand tall.
Find your voice, let it be heard,
Let them hang on to every word.
Find your fire from within,
Find your own light,
Allow it to shine bright.

You Are a Beauty More Than You Will Ever Believe

You are a beauty more than you can see;
You are a vision I wish to see in me!
A beauty you are with a heart so free!

Gia Schön

Tonight, I Choose to Shine Bright

Brighter than all the stars in the night sky—
I choose to wash my fears away,
Pick up all my broken pieces,
Choose to be a better version of me.
Some will criticize; I don't care.
Some will love; I thank you.
Some will be unsure; that is okay.
This is for me—not for any of thee!
My choice of how I wish to be
An inner strength stronger then ever before
The choice I choose is for a better me!

No Angel Was I

Trauma and anguish...
Difficult as it may be to open my heart to thee
Once so innocent and joyful,
To trauma and anguish
Where my pleas were deemed outlandish
Wallowing in sorrow and pain.
Finding comfort in an intoxicating sanctuary—
Such a pleasure came with ease.
Before I knew it, my fun was seized—
A downward spiral through the darkest hell
Trapped in one's own intoxicating jail cell.
Hark! I hear the toll bells ring;
Days of end soon came near
Till I heard angels whisper in my ear,
"Listen to what the Scripture has to say."
The dawn of a new day
Is not far away.
Strength in spirit
With good merit,
Believe in one's soul,
There is a higher goal.
Dawn of a new day,
Slowly watch your spirit soar!
Soon be told
Of the many lessons
Where I found my many blessings.
Gratitude I find—even in days I was once blind.
Louder and louder I began to hear my own inner roar;
Peace and tranquility
Soon were found.
While navigating my way to true divinity,
Silence had the loudest sound.
Dawn of a new day—
The new me is here to stay!

Hear the Rain Pitter-Patter

Clouds of gray really don't matter,
Skies above in beautiful hues.
Sun rays starting to shine through,
Step outside embrace the storm.
Dance in the rain,
Swim with the waves,
Show the world how you have transformed!
Even on the darkest days,
A shining light will find its way.

 Summer's Night Dream

Things may not be as they seem—
Touches and screams
How could this be?
Threatens, "insane" they will all deem.
It was a well-sought-out scheme;
A nightmare it was per diem.
Time has passed, regained my self-esteem.
Blinded all will be
As my inner me is set agleam!

Some Say She's a Psycho

Others say a devoted disciple…
The decision may be biased,
Others say a crisis.
People reacted hysterically;
Others acted mysteriously.
Truth be told, she is sane—
Only concealing a deep pain
Consisting of broken parts,
Including a shattered heart.
She stays true to her love,
Looks for direction from above,
Knowing she must let him go
For his love for her was a foe.
Slowly the heart will mend;
Angels from heaven will tend.
She patiently waits,
Leaving it all to God's fate.
Angels assure in abundance.
Rejuvenated with no reluctance
A heart of gold is her key—
Allowing it to unfurl,
Precious and resilient as a pearl.
The world takes notice, as a rare gem is she.

# Hearts of Gold

Covered in sorrow
Deep within, what once was radiant.
Clouded thoughts,
Storms of confusion,
Rainbows of hope,
Sunshine so euphoric,
All harbored within.
Golden hearts have a solid core;
Believe in you and let the gold shine through!

Why Does It Still Hurt?

I beg for strength.
I was doing fine...
Till you popped back in my mind.
Tears stroll down...
"Forgiveness," I plead.
Guidance within
Will never be dim.
Trust the light; it will steer you right.
As hard as it seems,
The hurt will not last.
See, forever it will be
A piece of me.
Remember the laughter—not the tears.
Remember the joy—not the fears.
Most importantly, feel the love;
Embrace the cheer.

Finally, at Peace of Mind

All were happy, so kind,
At peace... maybe you, tougher you would never find.
You were gifted;
The weight is lifted.
Full circle... you reached the most beautiful monument
Your heart is finally connected.

ark Clouds Pass in the Sky

Storms on the horizon...
The winds blow,
The silence eerie,
So many changes, so little time.
Take cover; it will be a rough ride,
Hold down the hatches,
As the storm passes.
Signs of items weathered,
The skies in its pulchritude,
Calmness in the air,
Twilight's rays...
Suddenly most familiar
A serenity there is within.

Flowers of Bloom

Like the morning dew
So fresh and new,
Flowers so gentle and pure,
Exquisite and breathtaking,
All the same—
Their claim to fame.
See the pain.
Feel the distress,
Queries remain.
Will I be picked, so they can enjoy—
Yet watch as I wither away?
Will they just touch
My delicate leaves
So fragile, please do not judge…
Will tear if not handled with care.
Look for eyes of wonder,
Just watch and ponder.
Beauty complete.

Enjoy the Serenity

This is where I am my best.
The insects nurture from me—
The ground of rain-filled soil.
Allow my roots to grow stronger;
Please leave me a little longer.
My leaves may be bruised,
My blooms may die;
Watch me be reborn from a new leaf.
Many stages am I—
As other parts die,
It allows me to become
stronger and free,
Prettier and blessed,
To ensure the world will see me.
My true beauty,
My strength,
My purpose,
My necessity—
No matter what the world throws,
I promise I will never allow it to defeat me!

Dawn of a New Day

Is not far away
Strength in spirit
With good merit,
Believe in one's soul,
There is a higher goal.
Dawn of a new day,
Slowly watch your spirit soar.
Soon be told
Of the many lessons
Where I found my many blessings.
Gratitude I find—even in days I was once blind.
Louder and louder, I began to hear my own inner roar;
Peace and tranquility
Soon were found.
While navigating my way to true divinity,
Silence had the loudest sound
Dawn of a new day—
The new me is here to stay!

ike Dragons I Breathe Fire

Pay attention as I am not for hire.
Watch as I soar the skies,
No more cries.
I listen to me
Not he or she.
Watch as I stretch my wings;
I will scare even the most powerful kings.
Soar the skies,
Clouds will hide,
To allow me to be.
I don't need anyone by my side;
Sit back and watch me fly!

Pain Within

Behind a smile hide tears of anguish
That are never vanquished.
Living a life of sin and deceit—
The heart no longer beats.
Shadows of eminent pain,
showing no signs of subsiding;
The feeling of ominous
Is dominant.
Conflict within
Does one just give in?
Voice of purity,
Say that is not a cure.
Negative thoughts will refrain;
Inner beauty will regain.
Build your confidence;
It will not stay anonymous.
The light will restrain
The shadows of eminent pain.

She Is a Special Beauty

So elegantly
Like a symphony,
She taught my heart a new vocabulary.
Eyes of sorrow
She will hide tomorrow.
She is so brave—
Buried emotions in a deep cave.
Shoulders so strong,
Yet getting weak knees.
There for everybody
Yet feels so lonely;
Her love so pure
Becomes everybody's cure.
Children so admire thee;
You hold their key,
A true luxury.
You are vibrant,
A soul so exuberant,
A true beauty queen
With heart of gold.
Truth be told,
You hold a heart that is gracious;
Nothing is more precious.
Your love is contagious;
You see, you are the world to me—
Oh, how I love thee!

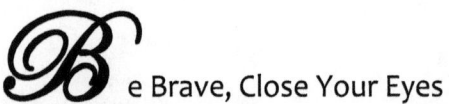
Be Brave, Close Your Eyes

Trust I am watching over.
Be brave, rest your head;
Trust I am defending.
Be brave, save your strength;
Trust my wings are your shield.
Be brave, let your heart be;
Trust I am protecting.
Be brave, as when you wake,
They will hear you roar
With A STRENGTH LIKE NEVER BEFORE.

The Heart Aches

As it breaks,
The heart aches
With pain.
The heart aches;
It cries tears of silence.
As delicate as a diamond
That sparkles bright,
The heart shines.
Trust me, my child, you have what it takes;
You have so much to gain.
Trust me, my child, I see your vibrancy.
Trust me, my child, allow me to guide you.
Trust me, my child, there is no stopping you now!
Allow me to help you
Shine bright, be your own light.
Trust me, child, as I am your heart!

ruly You

One morning you wake up and realize all is all right—
The hurt, the tears all subsided.
You will always remember and will never forget,
Yet know that your heart is content
Knowing that he is happy and in love—
Even when the love is not you.
In the end, all you truly wanted was for him to be truly happy—
No matter what the cost for you.
That is due to a heart that truly loves you!

earts on Fire

Heart aflame,
It will never be the same.
Hurt was disguised—
Once left for its own demise.
Set aflame;
There is no one to blame.
Tear it open;
Show you are no longer broken.
The darkness escaped,
Allow the light in to reshape.
Trust the warmth of the flame;
I promise this is no game.
Set the soul afire;
It is truly one's personal spire!

*L*earn to dance in the rain…

To enjoy the sunshine.
The darkest days may feel like too much pain;
The brightest day will prove you weathered the storm.
Find strength to fight,
Find your inner light,
Allow it to shine bright.
On the darkest days
When all you want to do is lay,
It seems like nothing is going your way.
Find the time to rest
To restore yourself to your best;
This is just another test.
Just be persistent;
Stop being resistant.
You are resilient;
Others will start to listen—
Not one of them is omniscient.
Believe, and the rewards will leave you incandescent.

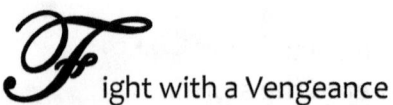

Fight with a Vengeance

Don't be blinded by ignorance;
Set the standards higher.
Follow your inner desires;
Prove you do not live in an ivory tower.
You hold the power;
Claim back what they stole—
Show you have full control.
This is your kingdom;
Fill it with your wisdom.
Take them under your wing;
Remind them who's King!

Soar Through the Skies

Fly high!
Spread you wings!
Let the heavens hear you sing!
Be as free as can be!
Leave all the burdens behind;
Release them from your mind.
Take a rest if required;
Others may stop to enquire,
Which may ruffle a few feathers.
Stay calm; always keep your eye on the treasure.
Fly high! Soar the skies
With elegance and grace!
Many admirers will embrace
Trust in the heavens above;
They will protect you with all their love.

est Decisions Come from the Heart

True intent and well blessings
Will always bring happiness to one's soul.
Although one may be sad, it brings on an inner glow.

It Tries to Let You Down Ever So Tender

As the heart surrendered
The mind in oblivion,
The voices got louder.
As one was left to ponder,
This was supposed to be with ease—
I beg, "Make it stop, please!"
Every breath
Felt like sudden death.
Frozen in my steps,
They all watch as I wept.
Trying to recompose,
I do not want to impose.
Gathering my thoughts—
Peace is what I sought.
One breath at a time,
Slowly I regain control…
No longer allowing this encompassing of my soul.
Fear will always be,
But I promise I will always overcome thee!

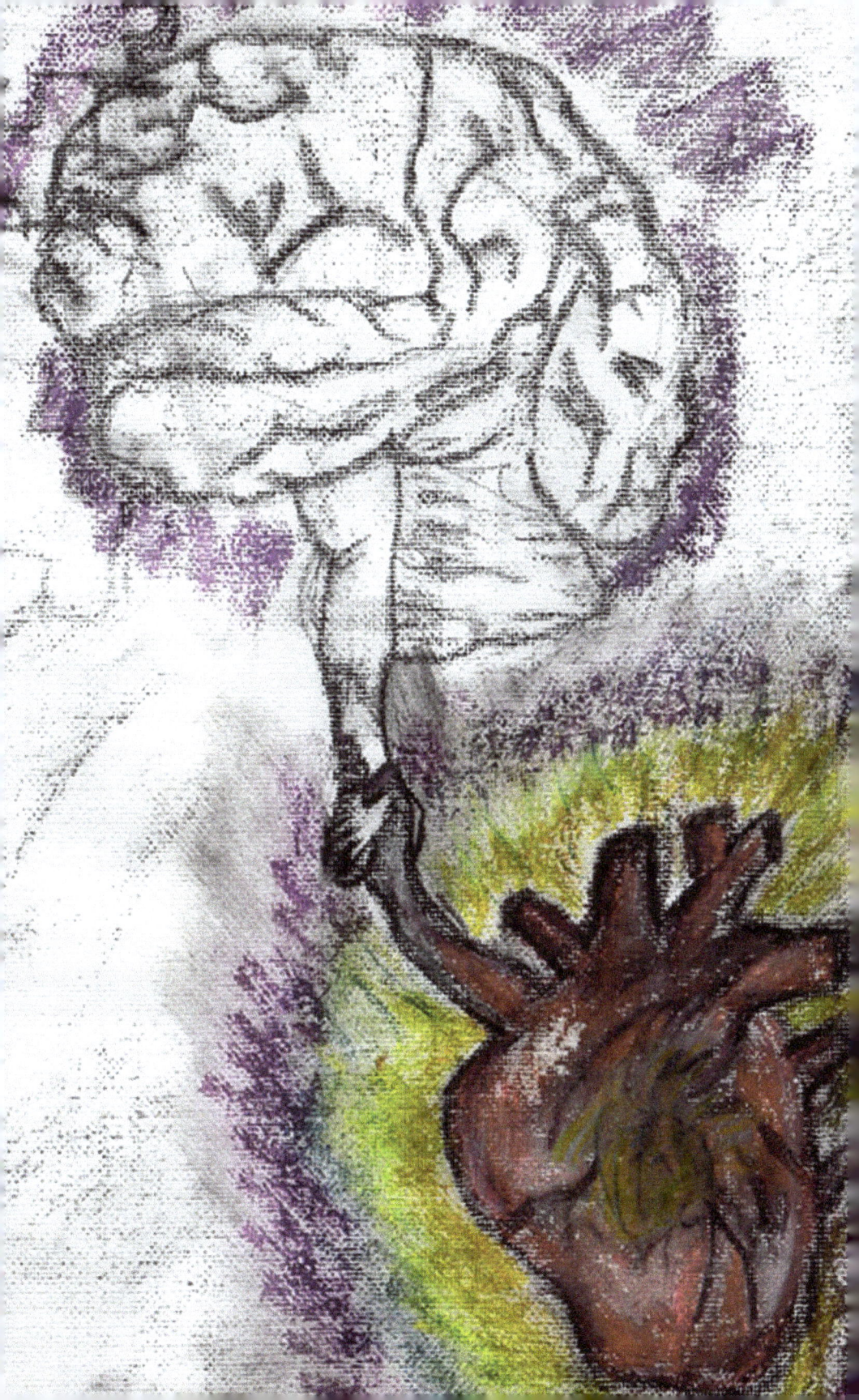

The Eyes Are Too Exhausted

They no longer see.
The mouth has retired,
Linguistics no longer an attribute.
The ears sound
Lost in their complex labyrinth.
The brain has shut down—
No longer allowing a fruitful thought.
The soul fought;
It was a good fight
Days are gloom;
No sun shines through.
The heartbeat pleads,
"Just one more last beat."
The soul whispers,
"Go ahead; give it one more try."
The heart beats
As loud and strong as could be.
The soul whispers a little louder...
"Again heart, one more time."
The brain pleads,
"Please let me go."
The soul shouts,
"Again heart, let's hear the beat!
Let's drain out that brain."
The heart beats rapidly,
Loud and vigorously
The soul screams and shouts,
"I have within one last fight!"
Without a second thought,
The heart beats once more.
The eyes awaken
And take notice of the world's newfound beauty.
The mouth, emeritus of linguists,
Starts to smile in awe.
The sounds of the ears

Gia Schön

Finally find their way through.
The days are brighter—
No longer gloom!
The brain is ecstatic
Yet once again!
The soul won
This last fight!
With gratitude to the heart
For never giving up!!

You Need to Care About You!

We all care; we truly do!
Once you change how you feel,
Those who don't belong will fall away.
Those who are true will stay at bay,
Believe in you, and all will come through!

Life Is Overwhelming!

It is all so depressing—
Mind is a blur
Feels like there is no cure.
Chaos is the new world order;
We are all just obedient soldiers—
Doing as we are told,
Fitting right into their mold.
It's almost robotic;
All is so psychotic.
Need to break free!
No one is hearing my plea—
"Someone, save me please!"
They come, but just to tease.
I now realize it's all up to me!
I can do this; I can break free!
Hard as can be, I fight—
Fight with all my might.
They tried to manipulate and kill my will;
They tried very loud and shrill.
I did not give in;
I assure you triumphantly I will win!
Free at last!
No longer part of their cast,
I broke the mold!
No longer doing what I am told,
I'm free to think on my own—
No longer one of their clones
With every breath of fresh air,
I solemnly promise, I will handle the new me with care.
The fight will always be true for one to defend,
But I assure you, I will fight for ME till the very end.

Today's Journey Has One in Tears

Left with all of one's true fears,
The body aches as the heart cried;
All the while the mind believed all those who lied.
Voices in one's head scream and shout;
Pandemonium broke out.
The memories are in disarray—
Trying to sort through them in every way.
Where does the truth lie?
Is all this mayhem due to lies?
Slowly working through it, hear the pitter-patter,
Only to realize it no longer matters.
What once was is no longer;
What will be is only allowing one to be stronger.
Old memories cordially invite those of new,
Welcoming each with a new view.
Mind and body finally found their peace and harmony
Step by step toward a new you!

Hearts Apart Make Some Grow Fonder

Hearts apart make others wish they were farther away...
At times it is proven hearts do ponder
One heart aches while the other awakes.
Both hearts had dreams and aspirations;
Both hearts had determination.
One heart knew they were never meant;
The other believed it was heaven-sent.
Trials and tribulations seem to hold true;
The hearts went down two very different paths...
One heart felt blue, all the while
The other tired of the wrath.
Near or away
Fonder or time to break away...
Till this very day, both hearts stand genuine
The lessons learned, the blessings divine.

The Abyss of Uncertainty

Holds the key to our destiny.
If one's not careful, even light matter
Is unable to defy gravity.
Choose wisely;
Fall deep or find the way through.
Rise as the stars of Lazarus!
Find your inner vermillion.
Set the sky ablaze;
Soar through with the inner power gifted upon you!

The Heart Will Never Comprehend

What the mind already knows—
Enlightenment is from within; it will help one mend.
See it through—even when at the deepest lows
On the rise.
You will see many birds fly…
As others will succumb to their demise.
One may fall after many tries,
Do not give up! Try again!
Do not believe the lies;
Like the phoenix, you will rise!

Feelings of Being Broken and Defeat

Causes all emotions to retreat!
Inner turmoil leaves one seething,
Causing difficulty in breathing.
Mind in oblivion
And the day is only in antemeridian,
Spiraled into a vortex
Within one's own cerebral cortex.
The battle may be frightening;
The end result will be enlightening.
One must allow the inner demons to die,
No longer listen to their lies,
No longer allow the memory flashes,
Allow them to burn to ashes!
You possess the inner power—
Even the faintest of hearts will feel empowered.
Rise from the ashes;
Your heart won the battle of the masses!
Show you can withstand the helix;
Rise above as you are the Phoenix!

nce So Good...

Turned out so bad—
Twist and turns,
Down a winding road of hurt and sorrow
To believing no point of living for tomorrow.
One day, the downward spiral
Started to unwind.
The days of rain became rainbow-filled skies,
A beauty beyond blows one's mind.
No more asking, "Why?"
Tomorrow came; it was no longer the same!
Cheer and happiness were heard in all that one had to say;
At that moment, it was known all was going to be okay!

ife's a Paradox

It keeps pulling from Pandora's box.
Demons no longer invade,
No more savage ways.
You no longer are their slave;
The Lord has heard you pray.
Trust in yourself, as you are extremely brave.
Follow your heart; it will guide you
For what is meant to be true.
People may mock,
Others may talk,
Do not allow them to push you down,
Do not even give them the satisfaction of a frown.
Rise above!
Powerful messages are sent through love;
Believe, and you will see
How beautiful life is truly meant to be!

The Brain Feeds Off What We Want...

The heart feeds off what we need...
The soul feeds off what we are meant to have...
Till all three are fed a dish with all three items,
Inner peace will always be in turmoil!
Nourish oneself to be healthy in mind, body and spirit!
Peace and happiness will be met!

Voice of Reason

There is one for every season;
Listen carefully.
They will guide you truthfully;
Believe in the voice.
It's not just noise
Guided from within;
The voice is one's inner twin.
You are stronger then you ever been!
Believe in yourself;
Stop placing it on the shelf.
Stand tall;
Do not fear the fall!
Be true to you;
The heart and soul will follow through!

ears Wiped Away

It is a new day;
Dreams of love have faded...
Inanimate wish
No longer in anguish...
A quondam lover
Once left to wonder—
No longer even a ponder.

Anxiety Setting In

The mind is in a whirlwind;
Fear is taking over.
It feels like a hostile takeover!
Then I hear the voices sing,
"Stay calm; I have you under my wing.
Trust it will all be worthy;
It is part of your journey.
Take deep breaths, just believe;
I promise feelings of reprieve.
Once thoughts of despair
Will soon be distant whispers in the air.
Believe in me as I do you."
Suddenly the heart calms,
No more sweaty palms,
The mind is suddenly at ease.
I apologize; I know it is hard to please.
Trust in my faith is a given—
As my trust in You is no longer hidden.

Life is Unpredictable

Just when you are comfortable,
Life sends you a twist.
You are left amidst—
Internal confusion,
Feelings of living an illusion.
Time will past;
This too will not last.
Silent thoughts,
A strength to be sought,
Life will emanate.
Trust in fate!

The Moon Still Shines

Even after the sunrise,
Skies of blue
Hide stars too.
Dreamers dream
Day and night, it seems.
Watch the birds soar—
Freedom felt in one's core.
Always be true;
Always be you.
Day or night—
Be your own light!

In Murky Waters, Beauty Is Found

Murky waters may surround you;
They are not what defines you.
Do not allow them to tear you down;
Stand tall, straighten that crown!
Forget the road once led,
Let the memories shed.
Follow the guided path
Of the divine high priestess;
She is the one to help glue back all the pieces.
The universe entrusted her to unlock all your secrets.
Like the lotus,
She defines peace from within.
She will keep you focused…
Allow the water to flow,
And you will surely glow!

Morning Dew Glistens

Watch the resplendent sun rise over the placid waters;
Listen as early morning animals sing.
The soul's asylum rejuvenated,
Life's distress and vexation have vanished,
The mind and body filled with complete quietude
Through the souls enlightenment Nirvana has been attained.

Skies of Gray

Wash all my fears away.
Dancing in the rain
Hides all the tears of pain.
Dance I ought
Till all the tears are fought.
And so, ensure better days
are here to stay.

The Soul Is Tired

The heart retired,
Laughter hides the tears.
Dreams no more
Nightmares haunt the core.
Awake all night
To avoid the demons' fight.
We sit awake, watching the night sky
Till it turns to morning light;
That's when the demons seem to rest.
Day goes by; one tries living it to the fullest
Yet haunted inside, knowing soon night will fall.
The body, mind and soul will want to rest;
Those demons will rise once again to call
The heart and soul.
I know the soul is tired
And heart retired.
Strength I plead from within
To beat the demons so they will be no more.
And end this vicious cycle.
We have so much to look forward to, so
Trust in me—your sprit will soar!

Eyes Shine, Yet I See Sorrow Inside

Smile so bright, it warms on the coldest of nights!
Yet I feel pain hiding behind—
Old and brittle,
Yet strong at the roots,
Limbs twisted,
Leaves changed, many fallen—
Yet still able to rebuild and grow,
Never giving up even on the hardest of days.
"How did you do it?"
I asked.
"Your reply was simple,
The earth grounded me,
The wind molded me,
The sun nourished me,
The moon shined beauty upon me,
The rain taught me,
The snow allowed me to reset.
As hard as it was, in some seasons
The lessons were clear.
If I wanted to grow, I needed to weather the storms.
All the elements had something to offer—
A lesson or a blessing
Had to learn from within.
As long as my roots were strongly grounded,
I was able to conquer any storm.
My eyes may be tired,
My smile hiding pain,
This so I never forget—
The lessons I learned.
The soul reminds me of the blessings I earned—
The hummingbirds and bees,
Beautiful flowers in the trees
Are just a few,
Yet none compare to the blessing of meeting you.

Hope Became Dreams

Laughter became tears,
Love became hate,
Beliefs became fear.
Trust in yourself—
No one else!
Allow the dreams to become reality;
Wipe away the tears.
Allow the hate to become understanding;
Always conquer your fears.
You are uniquely amazing and simply beautiful!
A soul that shines bright—
Brighter then any other light!
Stop placing it on dim,
Stop believing in the obstacles,
Believe in the opportunity.
Believe in you
As I do!
Believe you are right where you need to be.
I watch you dim the light;
Now it is time to switch it to bright.
Believe in the inner light,
Believe in the soul,
Believe the mind,
Believe in the heart,
Believe in you—
As I do!

Such Disdain

Left with so much pain,
The vibe inside
Attracts the tribe.
A lesson or a blessing,
The heart is professing.
I am a seed
To be nourished—a need.
Beautiful miracles form from dirt;
It will overpower all the hurt.
Watch me thrive
If one does not deprive.
What one reaps is what he or she sows—
The choice is yours for how you wish for it to grow.
A cause to reflect,
Do not neglect.
Blessings you will find
With a change of mind.
Catalyst growth of the Inner being
Will be freeing!

Gia Schön

Judge to Hide and Not Be Judged

Misunderstandings lead to hurt and sorrow;
One never knows what is hiding behind a smile
Or the meaning of a tear.
We are all individuals—all unique.
The war may be the same but every battle very different;
How we conquer the battle may differ from the other.
We deal how we know with what we know—
With the sources at hand
And learn in the process.
No two footprints are the same;
Do what is right by you, in your heart, in your soul.
Leave all others at the door;
They will comment and judge
They will disagree. Some even might agree
In the end. They are not fighting your battle;
They are not walking in your shoes
As you are not walking in theirs.
Welcome all to walk along—
Not behind,
Not in front,
But beside You
As you walk alongside them
As support and strength for one another.
Do not judge each other;
Just support one another.
This alone makes all battles just a little easier!
Help so we don't give up on us.
Help fight the battle at hand—
No matter how small or large;
It is your personal battle.
Some battles you win;
Others you will lose.
Both help build strength to win the war;
In the end, our wars are the same—
To find the Inner us
And to find peace, tranquility and strength!!

*O*nce blinded...

And misguided,
I promise to fight
Till I find the light.
Climb the tallest mountains,
Swim, the deepest seas,
Till I am found.
It will be profound;
I promise it will astound.
I will conquer—
Just wait and see.
Possibilities are endless
When I believe in me.

Gia Schön

I hold back tears—

Not because you are gone
Or because my heart was lonely,
But because I no longer trust anyone to confide in about my fears.
No longer have anyone to converse with till the break of dawn
Or because I no longer want anyone to hold me closely.
I hold back tears
Because I believed in love.
I believed in it for many years,
And all I believed it was conceived of.
I hold back tears
Because I realized I was broken.
I realized things are not always as they appear;
Many truths were left unspoken.
I hold back tears
Not because I lost you
Or because of all the promises whispered in my ear,
But because I once believed it all too.
Then one day the tears just let go;
There was no holding them back.
I just let them flow—
Just kept crying like a maniac.
I finally released the tears,
Found I was once lost and finally I was found,
Realized I was held back by all the fears ;
Time has come to turn my life around.
I finally released the tears
Stopped seeking love from others.
Realized I was a fool for many of those years
And never followed through with my own druthers.
Then one day there were no more tears;
I was no longer broken this I knew to be true.
The only whispers I now hear are those of great cheers
All because I finally learned how to love me too!

Let Your Inner Flame Glow

Never keep it on low.
You are a jewel in the night—
Shimmer and glimmer like no one's in sight
Be you, not who they want you to be
And shine bright for all to see!

They say the truth hurts…

But they never said what kind of hurt.
Maybe it's a hurt just because someone forgot how to believe.
We all worry about each other,
But we forgot how to believe in that one special person—
That person hiding inside of us—
The one as we all refer to individually as me, myself, and I.
Maybe if we just believe,
The hurt will be of laughter not cries,
The hurt will be tears of joy,
The hurt will be chest pains from love
We were embracing from inside!
Allow the truth to hurt from the pain of joy, love, and laughter!!

Thankful You Entered My World

Thankful for all the years we believed we were in love
Thankful for all the years of feeling loved
Thankful for the bad and the good
Thankful for the lessons taught
Thankful for teaching me how to love
Thankful for allowing me to feel
Thankful for making me believe I was wanted
Thankful for teaching me strength
Thankful I met you
Thankful you are now truly happy
Thankful for you!
Thankful you are who you are
Thankful I fell in love with you from the deepest part of my heart
Thankful you will always hold a piece of my heart
Thankful I learned to trust
Thankful we were broken apart
Thankful you are no longer a part of me!
Thankful, for without you, I would have never found me!
Thankful from the bottom of my heart!

Today Is the Day

To wipe away your fears.
Today is the day
To dry up all the tears.
Today is the day
Your heart has its true say.
Today is the day
You will find your way.
Today is the day
All will fall in place.
Today is the day
You no longer feel like you need to chase.
Today is the day
You will find the true you.
Yes, today is that day!!

You Truly are a Beauty

The need to remind you is my duty;
You know it is true way down deep.
Bring it to the surface, take the leap
Allow your eyes to see
what I see in thee.
No soul will ever be able to compete;
Listen to the inner you.
It has been silently waiting
And now it is ready to break through.
They have their own fears;
They don't know how to just be an ear.
Their Intent is well-meant—
Never with any Ill intent.
Truth is they have true admiration
And try hard to hide their infatuation
As they are amazed by your determination and soul's creations.
You are a beauty!
Believe, it is your duty.
Stop the self-doubt;
No need to continue to pout,
Allow the inner beauty to break out.
Believe I plead—
Believe in the planted seed.
It is undeniable
Your skills are viable;
Believe they are attainable.
The struggle is true;
We all deal with inner battles too.
Time has come to close the self-doubt door;
Time has come to end the war.
Your courage will be awarded in bravery and valor;
Inner beauty is finally shining through.
Never saw such a radiant glow—
Look at that beauty flow!
We are so very proud of you!

 elieve in You

Close your eyes,
Listen to your heart,
It will not feed you lies.
Trust the soul;
It will help guide you through.
Forgive the sin;
It will bring peace within.
Stand up for you
And others will too.

et the Imagination Run Wild

See beyond what everyone else sees;
Believe in your own intuition
And allow it to guide you—
Let it be in the cosmic realm
Or deep in the abyss.
Climb the tallest mountain
Or swim the deepest seas.
Trust in whom you are meant to be;
All you need to start is to believe!

Walk Side by Side

Not one in front, nor behind
Friends in laughter
And through tears
Sisters in times of need
Brothers when at war.
Stand tall, no matter at what stride,
All have personal battles in their mind.
Insecurity and doubt are one's captor;
We all have irreconcilable fears
Derived from an old seed
Planted deep within one's core
Help lift a hand; always be kind
We all have a strength
Followed by a weakness.
No matter the battle, it helps today for a better tomorrow
No matter how large or small.
Indestructible we are—
As long as together we stand.

Time to Stand Tall

I hear their taunting call,
I will not fall.
I am stronger than them all—
No longer allowing you to beat me down,
No longer allowing myself to frown.
I stood up once before;
I will do it once more.
My heart once worn
Is no longer torn.
No longer will I suffer—
Enough of this pain,
Enough of the tears,
No more running from my fears.
I have so much more to offer,
So much more to gain.
Stand tall I will;
This is a promise I will fulfill
till the very end.
Trust in me, I will defend.

Goodbye to those words,
I never realized came across as negative!
Goodbye to the thoughts that brought me down!
Goodbye to those who didn't want to understand.
Goodbye to those whose journey in my life has passed!
Thank you to those who supported me at my worst.
Thank you to those who walked away, which taught me to look deeper within.
Thank you to those who taught and forced me to learn many lessons.
Thank you to those who walk alongside of me as I travel on my journey.
Hello and welcome to all the blessings that are a result of all above!
Hello to a new life that has set the inner me free!
Hello to learning and starting to love me!
Hello to new beginnings!

Fallen, Yet Not Broken

On bended knee,
I pray to thee.
Hear the words I left unspoken,
Forgive the unforgiving,
Wash away the tears,
From all the world's fears,
Peace I pray for the living.
Trials and tribulations within one's core—
The things we do to numb the pain.
There is nothing left to gain;
I don't think they are able to take much more.
Let them see that you are there—
That you caught their fall.
So, once again they can stand tall;
Let them know we all do care
Angels they are, this they need to see;
They just took a detour.
See the pain they just couldn't endure
Now they plead on bended knee.
Strength from within,
Inner peace we plead.
Understand it is was not greed;
Forgive for all our sins.
"My angel, I hear your plea."
Angels soar from above
Feel the wings I descend to thee,
Hold your head up high.
I hold the answers to all your whys;
You must realize you are the angel I love.
Time has come to wipe away all those tears;
Set your wings free.
I will always watch over thee;
It is your time; "Soar high, my dear!"

Tears Allow Me to Stand Tall!

Do not condemn me for my tears!
You will never understand their bravery and stamina;
They do not stop me from challenging my fears.
Yes, I may have an insecurity or two
Which may cause me to shed a few extra tears too.
Crying is not my weakness;
Vulnerable is just not the case.
I feel from the heart
Though overwhelming it may be at times.
They ensure I recall my strength;
The strides I take are at exceptional lengths.
Crying releases my pain—
Allowing for bravery and fortitude,
Tenacity and humility,
An oath I choose to abstain.
Do not punish me for my tears!
My life prospects are not bleak;
Tears do not make me weak.
I do not hide behind a wall;
I admit to my falls.
I have remorse,
I feel others' pain.
My tears are the reason
I am able to stand tall!!
Never underestimate my fears or tears;
They assure mental fortitude.
My tears are the reason I am able to stand tall!

Sometimes We Just Sit in Silence

Sometimes we just hold one another without saying a word.
Sometimes it can just be a smile from across the room.
Sometimes it's the call, "Good morning!"
Or the one, "Good night!"
Sometimes it's a text saying, "Hi, I miss you!"
Or "You are a great friend!"
Whatever it is—
Whenever they would occur,
Sometimes it was just what helped someone get through another day.

Gia Schön

You Never Know a Loss Till You Lose a Loved One

Hold them dear,
Hold them near,
For days of love will soon be days lost.
Never regret,
Always reflect,
Hold onto the memories
For they will come upon you with ease.
A loved one lost is the hardest of them all.

ove to Sit and Talk

Love to hear your voice,
Love to see your handsome face,
Love to see you by my side.
I know you are not proud of me;
I know I made mistakes.
I know I was hard for you—
It was too soon;
It was not your time.
It was not right,
It was all fright.
Stay with me in my heart;
Please never let it go
Till one day we meet again.
Even if I just pass heaven for a second
And whisper in your ear…
For you to kiss my cheek,
To smile and say,
"I love you."
Tears flow
As I think of you.
My heart aches as if it were just yesterday…
How I miss you!
Till we meet again
In my dreams, you will stay.

isten to the Rain

The storm from the skies
As eyes of angels cry.
Don't worry, my child; it's not in vain.
Their death is pure, their soul in ecstasy,
With me they will be, by my side watching thee.
Smile and rejoice!
The storm is passing soon;
The sun will shine, and your heart will be fine.
Trust in me and the angels of the sky;
We love all the children as they are a part of mine!

Fear of Tears We All Shed

I will not stay! I am too afraid!
Run and hide, seek you will not find.
Shhh... I no longer want to play!
Tired is true, I need to find my way through.
Please understand, I no longer want to stand.
With angels is where I need to be—
In the sky of blue hopefully; the pain so agonizing.
My time on this earth has come to an end;
With Angels in the sky is my place to be.

Gia Schön

A Special Part of Me You Will Always Be

If I could I would take away your pain.
My heart cries like the thunder chimes.
My soul is heavy like a summer's rain.
My faith will guide me…
To where the river flows
To the garden of dimes
Where beautiful roses grow.
Beauty in three—
A thorn there may be.
The butterflies will soar the skies
As we stand united for thee.

We Might Be at Opposite Ends of the World

Yet the sky is connecting us closer than before—
A sea of sparkle
Waves from the core;
Look up at the stars
On this starry night to see
The star we wished on is so bright!
As night sparkles with light
Singing a sweet euphony—
Stars in their own harmony.
Feel the embrace,
The warm smile on your face,
The heart I hold
Is full of gold.
Soon the seas will swallow the sorrow
And breathe light for a new tomorrow.

Sometimes I Will Replay an Old Voicemail

Look at an old picture,
Sit and stare as I replay memories in my head,
Reminiscing of all that was said—
What a combination! some say even an odd mixture.
It was like a fairytale...
A land of hope and dreams,
A king watching out for his soon-to-be queen.
Then midnight came;
Nothing was ever the same—
Dreams shattered,
The heart was left battered,
A fairytale no more.
When the stars sparkle at night
My king shines down with all his might.
His presence felt
A warming in my heart that makes me melt.
Tears come to my eyes
As I take a deep sigh.
To see your face,
To be held in your arms,
To dream a dream.
Till the day we meet, and I can hear your voice once again!

Gia Schön

Angels Descend from the Heaven Above

To deliver a message to thee.
The earth transitions from dark to light
Instilled in thee the ability to shine bright!
As time has come you are ready to face
As the world is ready to embrace.
Talent from one's darkest days to the brightest night
Share among all in sight
Trust in me as I do thee.
Trust as I send my angels from heavens above
To watch over my greatest love.

Gia Schön

I Wish You Could Just Call!

To hear your voice even for a minute,
To have you hug me and say, "It will be okay,"
To knock on my door, say, "I am here…"
And open arms with a hug.
To cry and stay silent by your side—
Some days are harder than others.
I know you are there—
I look to the sky, and tears roll down my eyes.
To see your face in the clouds,
To hear you whistle through the birds,
To feel the warmth of your hug from the sun—
Nothing can ever replace a call—
Missing you!

Days of Sorrow

Make one believe there is no tomorrow,
The pain one feels is insane.
Mind wishes for days to end;
The heart pleads for it to mend.
Yet days of tomorrow
Are the only way to heal the sorrow.
It's days like today
One wishes the memories away.

Gia Schön

I**t's Been a While Since I Have Missed You Like I Do Today...**

To hear your voice just one more time,
To have you hug me and say it will be okay,
I miss the friend I once I had in you...

When the Soul Is Not Able to Speak

The eyes weep...
As tears flow.
The heart still aglow
With a glimmer of hope,
One will learn to cope.
The eyes speak
As the soul weeps.

Gia Schön

Lie at Night Quietly

I turn my head for her not to see
As I slowly weep
Till I fall asleep.
May have been years
But I still get tears.
Memories so vivid
Anger inside, I am livid.
It was too soon;
I still needed you!
So much to teach me…
So much still to learn.
I learned to deal;
I just did not feel.
I never learned to cope.
Trouble I caused,
I was such a dope.
Time it took to build inner strength and stay strong
Till one day, I met her—
True love at first sight!
I knew it was for sure;
My heart felt it with all its might.
She is beautiful, spunky, and free
Reminds me of qualities in you, don't you see?
I look at the heavens;
I know you are smiling from above,
Watching over protecting me.
My heart afire
My love for you ablaze;
It is not just a phase.
In my heart I will always admire—
A hero to me you will always be!

One More Day, That's All I Ask

See your smile and eyes sparkle
To hear the never-ending stories
Or sit in silence…
See your smile,
Feel your touch,
Hear your voice
Even for a minute,
Tears will flow when you go.
Selfish inside, will like to keep you by my side,
But I know it is not fair;
You are happier over there.
I promise to push my feelings aside
To just be held in your arms—
Just one more time.

Gia Schön

Tell My Heart it Will Be Okay

Tell my heart no one is meant to stay.
Tell my heart it will mend one day.
It hurts more today
Than it did yesterday.
It hurts in a horrible way!
I hope and pray
The pain will go away…
Till then, my dreams are where I wish they could stay.

Today is a Day I wish I were Able

To just pick up the phone to hear your voice.
To see you and get a great big hug and hear the words, "I love you!"
I miss our talks.
I miss the days you knew I was upset or hurt,
And you would just look at me smile
Or sit beside me to watch TV in silence.
Bring me a drink or a candy bar
To just let me know you were there.
I miss you so!
I know you are happy,
And it is selfish to wish you were still with me.
It's been so long yet the hurt is just as if you left me yesterday.
I cannot wait till the day we meet again
To tell you all my stories now.
I have so many to tell for a change.
The selfish me wants you by my side
The real me is happy you no longer are suffering and in a happy place!
To many more conversations in my dreams and prayers to heaven…
Till we meet again.

Today, I Miss You a Little More

It should be getting easier—
Not harder within my core.
When all came crashing down,
I felt you push away.
I struggled holding on;
I felt you were just keeping me at bay.
Mistakes I made, these I own,
I did what I did for my little boy blue.
He is my only born;
My heart was torn.
Heartbreaks feel like a stabbing with a million stakes!
After all that was said,
I knew it was just a teaser—
I was nothing more then just a pleasure pleaser.
I broke, I fell.
No worries, I will glue myself back together.
I promise the stories I will tell
Of how I was shattered and pieced myself together.

Poems from the Heart to the Soul

Gia Schön

wonder if…

I wonder… If I call,
I know you will not answer.
I wonder… If I wait,
You will not call.
I wonder… If I appear
In your dreams.
I wonder… If you are real
In mine.
I wonder…
If your heart aches.
I wonder…
If mine will ever be the same.
I wonder…
If…

As Time Goes By it Gets Harder

I miss your smile, your touch, your voice…
Even listening to all the words you would say.
That charm… oh, that charm.
Friends to lovers to strangers it became;
It would never be the same.
It kills me that we ended up like this!
Know you are very missed.
I'm sorry for all and any harm;
The guilt drives me insane.
My heart's in pieces…
Yet every piece holds a memory of you.
My dreams were shattered;
I am left so battered.
I wish for you a newfound love, happiness, peace and tranquility.
Know I'll break my heart a trillion times
To ensure yours is protected in its purity.

Gia Schön

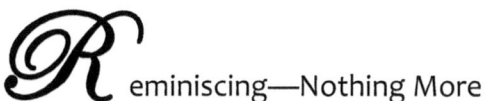
Reminiscing—Nothing More

Reminiscing of dreams no more…
Reminiscing about the good times…
Reminiscing about the sorrowful ones…
Reminiscing today of yesterday…
Reminiscing in hope of one day…
Reminiscing of a time before my heart ached.

Love Profound

Left one so unwound
Walls built
Came tearing down.
Touch the soul;
It takes a toll.
Heart weeps
Love buried deep
Forever will keep
Under lock and key.

Gia Schön

Some Days I Wish for a Sign

Others are just fine
If you seek,
What will you find?
Hardship and sorrow…
Bitter inside…
Built a love
So tender and sweet!
Once lost
Now am found.
Although I may wonder from time to time
The person I was
Has drastically changed!
What I now seek
Is no longer for you to be on my mind.

ove...

Lost...
Hurt...
Heal...
Trust...
Broken...
Love—
Never again!

Gia Schön

I Know I Am Difficult to Love

I know it is difficult for me to love,
But I will continue to improve.
And continue to learn my heart and my soul.
So one day, someone will love me truly.

# Many Faces of a Clown

What mask to wear?
To cover up Is a must
To build a false trust.
Many different faces—
Some of laughter,
Some of tears,
Yet there is a fear.
Scary, creepy,
Frightened indeed!
Hide within, or
Weakness will be perceived.
Morph into it—
A perfect fit
Allow one to adumbrate.
A charade?
Tell me, dear.
I will come to your aid!
What's hiding below
Deep within your soul?
Trust, hurt, laughter, tears
Anguish and pain?
Pretence of nurture
And care?
A true charm
could never mean any harm...
Enough to make one insane.
Hide and seek...
Do not peek!
Time for solitude,
Wipe away the laughter,
Wipe away the tears...
Reflections of all the years
Smile within
As they fooled again.

It Changed so Suddenly

Like a blink of the eye,
You say you were in love with her,
But then you met me.
Your world suddenly was seen so differently—
A love you felt like never before,
A warming in your heart, this time it was true.
If only my eyes could see what you see;
I would see how much I meant to thee.
My heart was guarded, it questioned, it doubted;
I shared the fear. You reassured,
You will always love me.
The walls came down
Little by little.
My love for you kept coming through
A personal battle from within.
Many faults I had I did not hide;
A heart so kind you were the one
I was meant to find.
At the worst of times—
Many chases, many fears
All accompanied with tears.
You would wipe them and say,
"As long as I am here, I will never allow a tear to roll down your face."
You promised me, "Forever together we will be
So very happily! See you loved me!"
But this wasn't the case…
In a blink of an eye,
It all changed…
You no longer were the same with me;
All the fears were rushing back.
Tears now rolling down over my heart
Felt like a knife in my back.

Gia Schön

The change was all so confusing;
You made me think I was going crazy—
I felt you no longer loved me.
I fought, I tried, I wanted to be with thee,
Yet you no longer wanted me!
You were back in love with her,
Fighting for her and not for me.
You say, "It's not true!" Did I not see
It was me who was pushed so far away.
I no longer was a part of you and me.
You loved her,
Then me—
Now you do not love any.
My worst fears came true;
The truth I do not know.
It feels like just lies to me—
Do you not see?
Yet my heart still longed for thee.

Gia Schön

Sky of Fire, Light Up the Night

Heart exploding in delight!
Flames of love
Fill the soul;
They make us whole.
My heart collapses,
Eyes fill with tears,
As I remember all the years
Never thought we'd end up here.
It was my worst fear
Like the fire in the sky.
My heart imploded—
Piece after piece exploded.

Awake All Night

Waiting for morning light...
I no longer sleep.
It hurts so deep—
Once dreams of you and me,
Which we now know will never be.

Hearts Grow Fonder

When they are no longer.
Sit and ponder.
As we listen to thunder,
Life makes you wonder
Why they never return their plunder.

Gia Schön

Thoughts have Passed...

They no longer last.
Memories fade,
No new ones being made.
No more tears,
I know you no longer care.
Heart was broken—
Just a prize token.
Mend it will, wait and see!
Erasing every part of who I used to be—
Soon just a memory of the past
Will be a reminder: nothing lasts.

he Sits in His Arms

Moving on so gracefully,
Found a true love the way it should be;
She never thought twice of the love it used to be.
I sit lonely and quietly
Reminiscing of the love once we had between.
Holding on to memories
Locked in my heart's vault even if only temporarily…
With hopes one day you will see my love
Was pure and sent from angels above.
My love is true;
It was beautiful just like you.
Memories within
Rekindle the flame once again.
Yet I know we will never be;
Your love has moved on,
You found your true one.
The heart never belonged to me…

Night Sky, Mystic Night

Gazing upon the moon,
Not a star in sight—
Sit and wonder
What is yonder?
Lost in thought
Not a sound is heard—
Not even the beat of the heart which is burred.
Wonder did we give it all our might?
Why did it end so soon?
Why was our love not worth the fight?
Mystic night—
Wondering why no star in sight...
The memories must be a haze;
Guess our love was just a phase.
This mystic night,
I wait till a star is in sight
To wish with all my might—
Fill the hole left in my heart tonight.

Wish the Dreams Were Real

They made me feel!
Seemed all surreal—
Held in your arms,
Head on your chest,
Caresses so gentle.
Hearts beat—
Perfect harmony!
Morning light
Wakes the soul;
Feel the bed next to me
Empty and cold.
A dream? How real it all seemed!
Try to fall asleep once again with all my might
To have just a few more moments
With you.
Lie just a few minutes,
Tears roll down,
The day must go on.
Countdown begins;
Night falls.
Soon I will be able to dream of you once again!

As He Lies Next to Her

Listening to her heartbeat,
Gentle kisses, oh, so sweet,
Holds her tight
And sleeps a peaceful night.
My heart skipped a beat;
It felt defeat.
As tears filled my eyes,
Started asking all the whys
With a tremor in my voice,
"Is she your choice?"
Not going to lie—
Wish it was me
Lying in your arms tonight,
Holding me tight.
The hurt unbearable—
Nothing comparable.

Total Dismay

What a start to the day!
Overwhelming inside,
A weight of unknown—
Like an avalanche on all sides.
Running to escape
The mind left agape,
Trying to see through the haze.
As the spirits guide us through the maze
With a force so tremendous,
A transition is upon us.
For inner tranquility
Seeking the abyss for complete serenity.

Time has Passed

Mind knew it would not last…
Love aglow,
The heart in overflow
Encompasses realms of the soul.
Written pages to one's own gospel—
Plethora of treasures,
No other love will ever measure.

ove so Catastrophic

It kills inside—
How could it be?
Something once so profound
Left the heart upside down.

Poems from the Heart to the Soul

Gia Schön

Awake in Mind

No peace to be found…
Thoughts running around,
Although once used to be tame,
No thought is ever the same.
Each one, like shattered glass,
Sprinkled in the grass—
Unable to pick up all the pieces.
No thoughts are cohesive
Exhausted from pain,
Some days feel insane
Some nights feel so confined
When awake in the mind.

Once the Mask is Off

You leave yourself vulnerable
Thinking that both are exposed and bare
Molded into one.
Once the mask is lifted, it is never the same...
Feelings are raw,
Then you realize he never took his off!

My Heart Cries

From the lies
Many promises made—
I watch them fade.
Truth be told,
My heart you will always hold.
My love was pure—
Of this I assure.
Your love for me?
I cannot speak for thee;
You decided we just weren't meant to be.
As much as it hurt,
I realize I am stronger without thee.
Thank you, my dear,
For all the joy and tears.
Wish you love in abundance from above,
Wish you find your everlasting love.

Love Today a Little More Than Yesterday

Love tomorrow more than today—
Love with sadness
Love with madness
Love with happiness
Love with might
Love and hold them tight
Love is always in sight.
Love to let go
Love a little slow
Love to be free
Love with glee.
Love to experience
Love is obedience
Love the deliverance
Love from your heart.
Love so it beats off the charts
Love to see
Love to set your heart free!

My Love Times Three

A little part of me,
A little part of she—
Gave us these three.
The eldest my first true love
A beauty no one can ever compare.
An old soul is she
Wisdom beyond her years to share
With a heart of gold
You had my heart sold.
Then came two—
A beauty nonetheless,
Free spirit and carefree
Love, joy and laughter.
What a gift is she!
Along came three
What a fight is he!
Stubborn and kind
With compassion
That blows my mind.
My three is the best part of she and me!
My three is all that fills a heart that belongs to me!
How you will never know how much I truly love thee?
My Love times three!

From the Day You Were Conceived

I couldn't wait to meet thee,
Joy and happiness overwhelming us three!
A belle you were so full of energy
With curls of gold
A smile that warmed in even in the bitter cold
Caring and gentle
Even when the rest of us go mental.
Intelligent and beautiful,
You are the star of my musical
Perfectly acoustical.
My belle you are—
As I am the beast near or far, but never the least,
You forever will be the belle to my beast.

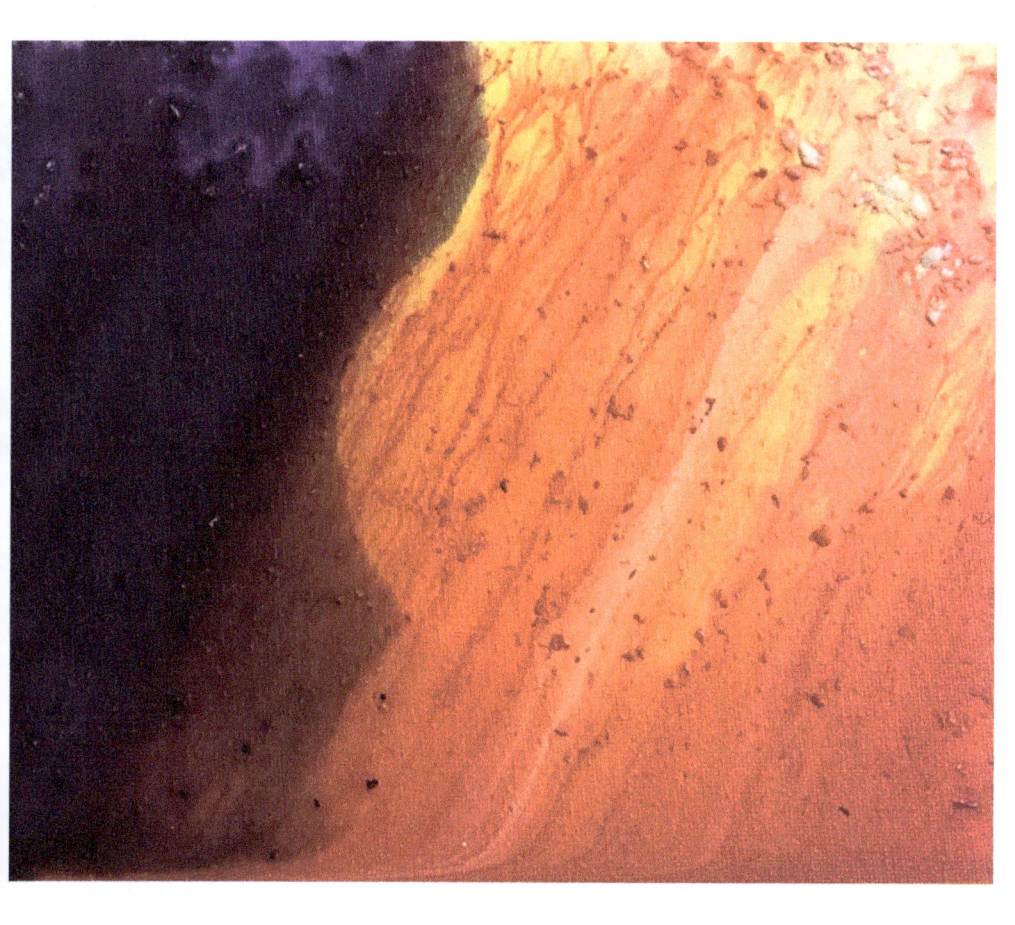

I Will Protect Him Till the End of My Days!

I will break my heart into a million pieces;
I will hand each one over one by one—
I will stop my heart from beating in me to ensure his always will.
I will forever and always place him before me.
I will always love him more than life alone;
You see, life to me is nothing without him.

Today I Was Reminded why I Was so in Love with My First True Love

His smile,
His eyes,
His hugs,
His undeniable wit,
His unconditional love,
He was my everything.
He still is my all
And forever will be.
I never would have imagined
How much love I could have felt for him;
It was instant from the moment I saw him.
The moment I hugged him I knew!
I just knew it was him!
And forever grateful that he was brought into my life!
Forever blessed and grateful I am honored to call him my son!

From Children to Adults

Family to friends,
Our journey will never end.
So gentle, so kind,
A beauty brighter than the sun shines.
With water between our toes,
Nobody will ever know
Every time we look at the sky
The memories you gave us... oh, my...

Gia Schön

ull of Love is She

A star in the sky does not shine as bright—
Her heart is pure, yet full of sorrow.
She is strong for others, yet weak inside;
Everyone else is her priority.
I watch her suffer;
I watch her plead,
Yet she will not give herself seniority.

Sometimes when Words Cannot be Verbalized

Our eyes see for the soul,
A hug feels for the soul,
A kiss will speak for the soul.
Our bodies entangled become one soul!
These are the words that speak for those that we cannot describe.

A Fool's World

Somber and sweet,
Let's pretend tears of joy
As our heart and soul's weep.

City of Two Spires

Opulent in gold and art
With an enchanting history,
Moonlight waters glistening,
Wind whispers sounds of Mozart
Filling many hearts' desires.
Let our hearts dance in Prague!
Hear the music play,
"The orchestra of love," they say.
Let's walk the bridge
Where the river flows,
As we listen to the winds whisper
Smetana's "Má Vlast" in our ears.
Walk hand in hand—
As our hearts dance.

Who Would Guess?

Odds they say are we;
Must have been fate.
A perfect match in harmony—
You are the yin to my yang.
As years go by
Days of commune—
They couldn't come too soon.
Left us with many things to ruminate
As I have gone astray;
You stay
Patient and kind,
Share words of wisdom—
"Life is short, be happy, love you."
Journey in life so eloquently
Defiantly, one of a kind
Though blood not are we.
Humble as can be
It is a great liberty
To say, "You are my family!"

Poems from the Heart to the Soul

Gia Schön

Witching Hour is What They Call It!

It is so unsettling; a candle is lit.
Walking around ever so quietly
Kids asleep snuggled so happily...
Our angel unsettled
She sits—just watching,
Then she barks.
A visitor must be lurking.
I return to my slumber
To see the telephone flash.
I grab it in a dash.
Who can be calling at 2:19 a.m.?
A voicemail left, yet no number missed—
Was it you?
Could it have been a message for heaven above?

# A Summer's Angel

Like a bright summer's day,
A spirit so free,
A smile so sweet,
A heart so pure with every beat.
Love the laughs,
Never lose that spunk,
Never lose the charm—
Many memories one will cherish.
You will always be special to me;
A summer's angel to me you will always be.

reek Goddess

Glamorous, gorgeous,
Compassionate and sweet,
Sparkles and shine,
Delicate and kind,
Radiantly dazzles,
Glimmers full of vitality,
One will never know how much worry or anxiety.
It was a catastrophe—
So full of agony,
A venture concurred so gallantry.
Heavens above watch over;
The gods are left breathless.
Nor diamonds, rubies or sapphires
Are as precious
As this Greek goddess is gracious.

We Met by Chance

Friends at immediate glance,
Laughter and tears,
Talked about all our fears,
Consoled each other when in need—
A friendship that created our own personal creed.
As all, we had our issues,
Went through quite a few tissues,
In the end our friendship proved its resilience—
A friendship with an extraordinary brilliance.
Friends became family so very naturally,
Friendship pure of love, has our heart leaven.
Friends are angels sent from heaven;
We can never measure their imperial worth.
So grateful the heavens sent you to this earth!

Nerves are Unwinding

Nothing is able keep them binded.
Pulse racing,
Unable to stop the brain from pacing,
Deep breaths.
Feel like dying a slow death.
Calming of the mind
Is so difficult to find.

Watching the Storm Roll In

The earth shakes
As the thunder quakes.
Lightning strikes
Light up the night sky.
Admiring the earth's beauty,
The mind is mesmerized.
Lost in thought,
Blissfully peaceful,
Silver lining on the horizon.
Rainbows suddenly fill the sky
Simply graceful!
A peace within
Knowing the storm's passed.

Beauty is Bestowed Upon Us

Never have to look too far—
Heaven above and Mother Nature are always on par.
Look up in the treetops
Or gaze upon the horizon…
We are surrounded by beauty;
Mother Nature is always on duty.

Gia Schön

Traveled the World

Many countries left my heart unfurled,
Sending my chakras into a whirl.
Happiness was found,
I finally belonged, I found my ground.
Then it was time, I was homeward bound,
That's when the battles started in my mind.
I searched but unable to find
Any words to be kind.
Constantly feeling I let all down,
Internally, all I do is frown—
If only I can run myself out of town.
No one understands
The battle I hold in my hands.
Everyday, tarnished thoughts seem to expand—
A satire of cynicism and self-criticism.
I search for the algorithm,
So the mind does not end in cataclysm.
Music is my solitude!
Forever will have my gratitude;
It takes me on a personal rendezvous.
My soul yearns,
My heart begs for many returns,
The brain just turns.
I know I can no longer run;
I am the only one
Who can find my inner sun.
I will shine!
My inner strength will be divine—
Once all the chakras will again realign.
I believe,
I believe in me,
I believe in my dream!

True Soul, You are Shining Bright!

Radiant in the night light
A soul so pure—
The finest line in haute couture.
A blessing you truly are,
No matter near or far.
As our souls connect,
I hold the deepest respect.
A friendship so truthful—
Forever I am grateful.

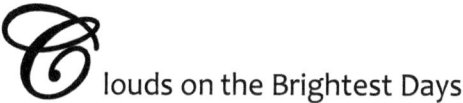louds on the Brightest Days

Fill the sky with beauty and delight,
Stormy days bring clouds of wonder that make us ponder.
Clouds of mind, body and soul
Ensure that one is truly whole.

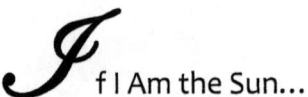

If I Am the Sun…

Will you be my rays?
If I am the moon,
Will you be the stars?
If I am the ship,
Will you be my anchor?
My eyes only look for you;
My heart beats just for you.
Every breath I breathe is just for you;
If I were to die, know I will die for you.

Hold Me Close, Never Let Go!

Love the way you kiss my soul,
Hold me close, never let go.
You are the glue to my heart's broken pieces,
Hold me close, never let go.
The world is crumbling beneath me,
Hold me close, never let me go.
My world is perfect as long as
You hold me close and never let me go.

Being Without You is Like...

A clock with no hands,
A lighthouse with no light,
The night with no sunrise.
Being without you
Is endless days and sleepless nights,
Living a life with no meaning.
To be without you... I'd rather not live.

Sometimes when Words Cannot be Verbalized

Our eyes see for the soul,
A hug feels the soul,
One kiss will speak for the soul...
Our bodies entangled will become one soul!
These are the words that speak volumes.

Velvet Kiss

A kiss so soft—just like velvet,
Touches ever so gently;
From my head to my toes,
Who would guess one can be so indulgent?
Fingers run through your hair,
Whispers of sweet nothings play in the air.
Feel the exhilaration,
With such admiration.
Take one's innocence,
With such vehemence.
A furiousness awakens;
Ecstasy felt in every fiber of one's being—
Complete euphoria!
Who would have guessed
Such bliss started with just one kiss?

Gia Schön

Sunset Over a Summer's Mist

Entwined lovers' tryst—
Subtle touches as they ravishingly kissed.
Waters calm, tranquility found
A beauty so profound.
Skies of pink, proof the hearts link
As lovers tryst over a sunset mist.

Star-filled Night

Like glitter in the sky,
Beauty beyond what one can imagine—
So peaceful and quiet...
Sit and let's reminisce of the days gone by.
Shhh, my love,
Enjoy the silence;
Let's just be.
Sit with me, by my side in silence;
Look at the star-filled sky—
The stars will touch your soul.
Listen as the waves of the water hit the shore,
Let them fill your heart.
Breathe deep, fill your lungs ... the air so pure,
Now, my dear, you hear that...
Shhh...
That, my dear, is the beauty of the world.
Shhh...
Did you hear that?
Then she turns to me to say, "But, my love, you say for me
To listen to the earth...
Yet all you do is stare at me.
That, my dear, is because to me you are my world!

Gia Schön

Astonished in Love

Enchanted by trees with leaves of color,
A warm breeze felt in the dim sunset glow,
Toes in the sand, watching the waves crash—
The effervescent of the water flows.
Nature so exquisite,
Enchanting to the eye.
The soul enchanted in tranquility
Leaves us all astonished in love.

My Dragonfly!

You make my heart sing;
Your spirit I hold under my wing.
A positive transition you will face
With elegance and grace.
Follow the music to the light;
I will always be in sight.
With an affinity of love,
You will always be part of my trinity
For all eternity.
The song you sing is played on my heart's strings!

Gia Schön

Sensual Love

The soft whispers in the ear
Make me bite my lower lip just a little harder.
Your whispers make my body shiver
As your fingers slowly caress every inch, every curve
Slowly, yet ever so gently, teasing.
My hands rustle through your hair.
The bodies entwined—
Passions make the mind wonder.
Glare in each other's eyes glisten.
Feel every inch,
Every thrust!
You make the body moan—
Sensual love ….
Wanting more
Intensity of the pleasure
Makes one want to scream!
Sensuality took over my every being
Our hearts beat in sync;
You seduced my soul.

Gia Schön

Eyes that are Mesmerizing

Lips so voluptuous,
A scent hypnotizing,
Skin delicately soft,
Gentle to the touch
Whispers of sweet nothings in the ear.
The body so imperfect, it is perfect.
A heart and soul so exquisite
It all makes me quiver.

erves Quiver....

His whispering suggestions make her body quiver;
Make no mistake, he was sure to prove he was a striver.
No man on Earth can resist the temptation to touch,
The urge just became too much.
Caress her every inch, her every curve;
The sensation will awaken every nerve.
Yet to allow one to be patient,
Thoughts may prove to be sordid;
Yet patience will be rewarded.

Intimate Love

So entwined,
Hearts in sync,
Passion in each other's eyes.
So intense,
Lips longing for the kiss,
Every thrust sends a rush.
The soul takes over;
Bodies become one.
Stare into each other's eyes.
Touch so gentle—
Skin on skin.
Then the moment longed for—
The kiss!
Gentle, yet forceful.
Delicate, yet adamantine.
So passionately,
So intense,
Every inch quivers,
Melts the soul—
Just want to explode!

It Took Just One Look

I knew it was you!
It was kismet
For us both—just us two.
There was no need to fret;
Our hearts were secured in
A love so compelling,
A love that was true.
Near or far, no matter where you are
My heart will follow,
As my love for you is worth telling!

Our Ears Hear the Silence

Of words that were never spoken.
Our eyes show one's truest emotion.
The sense of smell allows for the best memories;
Touch is the sweetest talk.
A kiss on the lips leaves us with the sweetest taste;
Intuition will never steer you wrong—
The heart feels the truest love.
Our senses will always guide us through love;
Always believe!

So Peaceful

Feelings of tranquility yearning from within,
The soul wistful of peace from all its sins.
Sometimes it feels better to bring life to an end
Than we glance outside
With tears in our eyes.
A message from the heavens above begin to descend—
Powder-covered branches
A reminder of all the past avalanches
An overwhelming calming desire,
Slowly puts out the inner fire.
Powder-covered earth
Encompasses one's girth—
A reminder of your own self-worth.
All powder-covered—
A time for one to hibernate,
Allows the inner being to be rediscovered.
When you re-emerge, an astonishing rebirth would have occurred!
It is never too late—
Trust in faith; this journey is part of your fate.

uide my Ways

Lift me up when I am down—
Strength to carry on,
Understanding of all,
Forgiveness for my soul,
Love when I think I cannot love any more,
I place my trust in you.
Amen.

Snow Freshly Fallen

Nature's beauty, which once was forgotten,
The wind blowing crisp new air.
One can sit for hours lost in stares
Reminiscing of days past
Or wishing on future days at last.
Then the mind goes blank
As one simply enjoys the fresh fallen snow-covered banks.
Beauty of white powdered bliss
Like heaven sent Earth a kiss—
Tranquility, Mother Nature's specialty!

aith

My knees may be weak,
But I know you are by my side to help lift me.
My shoulders heavy with burden,
But I know you will help exonerate.
My head full of confusion that is arduous,
But I know you will ensure it will soon be pellucid and bright.
My heart is in agony,
But I know you will comfort.
Many times, I fell
But I felt you catch me.
Many times, I didn't want to get back up;
That's when I felt you carry me.
Many times, I just wanted to shut the world out—
That's when you showed me its beauty.
Nothing but the darkness within;
You let the light shine in!

Today, it is Overwhelming

The feelings I hide…
Is that your heart I hear cry?
Wish I could wash away your pain…
Trust in the Lord as He will keep him safe.
Trust that the Lord took him peacefully;
He will be watching from above, protecting thee.
Look up! He is watching from the sky!
Close your eyes when you cry,
Feel the warmth of the flame;
That is him saying, "My son, I am here in your soul!
I promise; I will never let you go!!"

Support, Love, Trust…

Come in many ways.
In a dark place we were,
Looking for help
Out of the mind's crazy maze.
Last hope for some
On the verge…
Solitude, fear
Like the brain filled with sludge.
We just did not see clear;
Just get us out of here.
A voice calming and bright—
Words of encouragement,
And we started to see the light
You became our courage;
We were all profound.

Being in Love versus Loving Someone…

Loving someone is sweet,
They always have a special place in your heart.
Being in love with someone
Makes your heart skips a beat!
You smile every time you see that person from the corner of your eye;
You will move heaven and Earth to keep their heart safe!!
If you are in love or ever have been,
That is the most amazing feeling in the world!!

*i amo!*

Ich liebe dich!
Jag älskar dig!
Seni seviyorum!
Volim te!
Minä rakastan sinua!
Je t'aime!
Aloha wau iā 'oe!
I love you!
No matter the language; they are still
Three of the most beautiful words to be said.
But my favorite language is that of the body—
How my heart skips a beat when I think of you!
How my eyes fill with joy when they see you!
How my lips quiver when you are near!
How the body longs for your touch,
To be held in your arms.
All I want is to be with you!
See this is my favorite language of the three most beautiful words:
I love you!

Standing Tall,
Ready to fight
Resolute with prayers…
Many may be accompanied with tears,
But I promise to fight
Any and all battles that come my way.
I will fight with pride,
I will fight with dignity,
I will fight in honor.
I promise should I fall
To once again stand tall,
Regroup and resolute.
I will fight all battles the Lord sends my way
In honor of His name.

Gia Schön

At Times it May Feel Like Your Life is Like a Boomerang

You were held onto for so long then released
Only to return where you began,
Feeling confused, defeated and not understanding why.
Then it was like a lightbulb was turned on...
I am not where I started!
I was released; I was set free!
On my travels I was awakened.
I climbed the tallest mountains,
I saw the deepest, darkest valleys,
I swam the turbulent seas,
I weathered the roughest storms,
I witnessed the most picturesque rainbows,
I observed the most exquisite sunrises,
I experienced the peaceful night skies,
I found peace in my loneliness,
I found love from within—
I found me!
To be back where I started is false;
It may look familiar, but the difference is me!
So as those feelings from the beginning—
Defeat, hurt, rejection, loneliness, loss and confusion—
Start arising once again,
I lay you to rest once and for all!
May those feelings all R.I.P.
I am no longer the person you once knew;
I may look the same externally,
But internally I am a whole new person.
I am now whole!
I found my inner voice, my inner strength,
My passion, my love for life...
I found me!

Gia

This is Me

The sun shines.
As the water flows,
The moon still glows.
The trees may be in slumber,
Vibrant or full.
Every day a new beginning,
Every night a new reflection,
Time allows for one to be found.
Some say harsh words
Some speak beauty.
I am Me! A work in progress!
I try to smile everyday—even on the worst of days
Cause every day I either learn a lesson or receive a blessing!
Both work towards self-growth!
One thing I know without a doubt is I will always continue to grow;
I will always continue to learn!
I work hard and will continue every day to be better today than the person I was yesterday.
This is me!
All that matters is you believe in you
As every flower is unique!
This is me:
Some days are good;
Some days not so much.
Every day is a struggle to believe—
But never give up!
Learn to love yourself;
Everyone has an inner beauty that makes them unique!
Be true to you; this is the true me.
Everyone is beautiful = "Schön"
I am Beautiful Giacona = Gia Schön
Gia Schön = Yolanda Giacona
....This is the true me.

www.ingramcontent.com/pod-product-compliance
Lightning Source LLC
Chambersburg PA
CBHW070536090426
42735CB00013B/2996